Reflections on
the Spirituality
of Gregorian Chant

Reflections on the Spirituality of Gregorian Chant

Dom Jacques Hourlier

New Edition Revised, Expanded and
Translated into English by
Dom Gregory Casprini and Robert Edmonson

Series Editor
Dr. Richard J. Pugsley

PARACLETE PRESS
Orleans, Massachusetts

Third Printing, June 1995

Acknowledgements

*Special thanks are due to Mrs. Patricia Buckley Bozell
for her corrections and helpful suggestions
during the preparation of this English language edition.*

Table of Contents

Introduction

The *Entretiens sur la spiritualité du chant grégorien*[1] or *Reflections on the Spirituality of Gregorian Chant* was originally published in French as a memorial honoring Dom Jacques Hourlier shortly after his death in an automobile accident in 1984. The volume consisted of five lectures given by Dom Hourlier during a youth seminar on Gregorian chant spirituality held at Solesmes in August 1976. It also included two chapters on the more general topic of musical and liturgical spirituality, drawn posthumously from the author's notes.

Dom Hourlier worked on these texts with no thought to publishing them, and the French edition appeared with virtually no modifications in order to preserve the spontaneous character of the seminar lectures. For this reason alone, a straightforward English translation would be difficult. But there are other reasons as well. Dom Hourlier's audience was already well grounded in many of the basics of Gregorian chant and Catholic spirituality; moreover, the bibliography to which he constantly referred is not easily accessible to English-speaking readers. Thus, the English version is in fact a *revision* of the original work, along with some explanation of Dom Hourlier's thought. The last two chapters have also been revised; in the final chapter, quotations and commentaries have been added to stress the connection between Dom Hourlier's concept of the liturgy and that contained in the Vatican II "Constitution on the Liturgy."

Dom Hourlier was a renowned expert on Gregorian chant notation, spending long hours poring over manuscripts in the "paléo," the study room where Solesmes' chant archives are kept. He was more scholar than musician, not being gifted with a beautiful voice. But he took part in the monastic church services with an enthusiasm and joy that reflected a deep prayer life, nourished by the word of God. This prayer life became evident in his warm hospitality, something no one—music student or other guest—will ever forget. It also enabled him to speak with authority and wisdom on the subject of Gregorian chant spirituality.

Indissolubly linked to the Latin prayer texts used in the Catholic liturgy, Gregorian chant is an irreplaceable treasure of our human and Christian heritage, a truly "ecumenical" witness to the undivided Church. This liturgical music is not a mere external ornament, judged according to whether it "gets in the way" of prayer. On the contrary, it is so intimately related to the prayer-texts that it has become integral to the liturgy.[2] Alongside such monuments as the writings of the Church Fathers, Gregorian chant constitutes a *locus traditionis*, that is, a place in which Catholic Tradition is embodied, a built-in commentary or musical illustration of how Holy Scripture has been prayed and understood in the Church throughout the centuries.

Singing the chant requires self-abnegation and obedience to the Word of the Lord. Listening allows us to grasp the deepest meaning of the sacred words; it can carry us beyond all words and concepts to the very threshold of God's inexpressible mystery. It can thus lead to conversion to God in the most basic sense of the term, *conversio ad Deum*,[3] to a place where we experience silence and awe in the face of Divine Majesty.

This, in a few words, is Dom Hourlier's concept of Gregorian chant spirituality. His ideas, though conveyed with serenity, were a sort of protest against the iconoclasm, which in the wake of Vatican II was seeking to ban Gregorian chant from the liturgy for being obsolete and useless—notwithstanding the praise lavished upon it by the council. Today, the effects of this iconoclasm are felt everywhere. Despite popular interest, despite an ever-increasing longing for the most authentic and beautiful in sacred music, Gregorian chant is not only neglected, but attempts to reintroduce it are sometimes met by prejudice and ignorance. Dom Hourlier's message is therefore as relevant now as when he first delivered it. It is an urgent call to preserve and transmit to future generations this splendid Catholic heritage.

Dom Gregory Casprini
Abbaye Saint-Pierre de Solesmes
ALL SAINT'S DAY, 1993

Endnotes

[1] Editions de Solesmes, 1985, ISBN 2-85274-097-4

[2] cf. Vatican II, Constitution on the Sacred Liturgy, nos. 112 and 116. "The sacred tradition of the universal Church is a treasure of inestimable value, greater even than that of any other art. The main reason for this pre-eminence is that, as sacred song united to the words, it forms a necessary or integral part of the solemn liturgy . . . The Church acknowledges Gregorian chant as specially suited to the Roman liturgy; therefore, other things being equal, it should be given pride of place in liturgical celebrations."

[3] *Conversio ad Deum*—This Latin expression, which translates literally as "conversion to God," has an even stronger meaning in St. Thomas where it implies the turning of one's entire being towards the Lord.

1

A Survey

We are gathered here today out of love for Gregorian chant. We are striving to experience the treasures and joys that it offers, to sing in unison and to improve with practice. Together we aspire to savor and reflect upon the spiritual message contained in Gregorian chant. Our ultimate goal is to be able to praise the Lord in a deeper way.

This Gregorian session belongs to you. My only wish is to serve you. That is why I thought that the best approach in discussing the spiritual values intrinsic to Gregorian chant was to have you speak for yourselves. Thus I gave you written questions concerning the character of Gregorian chant, and asked you to jot down your thoughts and impressions about the way the chant affects your spiritual life. Your replies, ranging from simple notes to formal essays, stand out more for their quality than for their length.

Your thoughts can be grouped under three headings:
—Gregorian chant as education
—Gregorian chant as prayer.

—Gregorian chant as a way of life.

Let us go over each of these points, and then examine why and how Gregorian chant has all three characteristics.

But before beginning, it is interesting to note that many people today seem to be interested in Gregorian chant. This includes people of every age—young as well as old—all people of good will. Of course, there are here and there a few "fuddy-duddies" who hang onto Gregorian chant from routine alone. (I shudder to think how they must sing it!) But most of those drawn to the chant love it because of the way it benefits the soul, or more simply because of its beauty which they perceive with greater or lesser clarity. They are aware, if even only vaguely, of its spiritual value. This was illustrated to me recently by three Japanese women who on a visit to Solesmes said, "We are interested in Gregorian chant, not only because of the marvelous music, but even more because of its value as prayer."

When youth groups like your own meet, their primary purpose is generally to *sing* the chant. But your reasons for being here are much deeper than that: you meet not so much to sing as to pray, or, better yet, to pray in and through your song. Gregorian chant is for you a privileged form of prayer. You are drawn to it because you perceive the link between music and the sacred, between beauty and truth. With Saint Benedict's "instruments for the art of the spiritual life"[1] in mind, you wish to add a new "spiritual tool" to his list, Gregorian chant, which interprets your prayer and actually inspires it. And of course prayer implies union with God.

In all the above, as also in what follows, I am doing no more than coordinating your own reflections, in most cases retaining your exact expressions.

Gregorian Chant as a Means of Education

Gregorian chant is an important means of education because it binds the chant to the Latin word and to the idea expressed by that word. Quite often, one word was chosen over another simply because it was more suited to being sung. The chant, moreover, tends to give each word the fullness of its meaning through the construction of the melody.

Let us leave to specialists such detailed comparisons as the different ways the Introits for the First Sunday in Lent and Easter Sunday treat the Latin word, or examinations of the uses of the word *servus* in the different Masses. In these areas, the Biblical scholar must assist the Gregorian musicologist, just as the musicologist is needed to complete the work of the Biblical scholar.

I will also leave to these same specialists the pleasure of analyzing in detail this or that prayer text in order to show, for example, how the composer treated the text from Isaiah in the *Puer Natus* Introit for Christmas day, or the thrill of discovering in the Communion from the Mass for Holy Martyrs, *Et si coram hominibus*, an entire homily about suffering.

Instead, I wish to examine the chant from a more general point of view. As one of you remarked, in Gregorian chant, the music carries us far beyond the word. "You can look up the meaning of the words *lux* and *fulgere* in the dictionary, but the Introit from Christmas Mass of the Dawn, *Lux fulgebit,* transports you a thousand leagues beyond the dictionary. And the word *Magnificat* would be quite insignificant if the music did not make it the Song of Our Lady."

Through its capacity to take the listener beyond the surface meaning of the words, Gregorian chant truly expresses the way in which Church Tradition reads the Scriptures and writings of the Fathers. It is a vehicle of Tradition and an authoritative point of reference for theology, since it brings out the proper meaning of the sacred texts that are sung in the liturgy.

Gregorian chant can reveal, even to someone who does not know Latin, the underlying idea that governed the choice of a given text and inspired its melody. You yourselves said this using almost exactly the same words, in describing an experience in many ways similar to something mentioned by the great mystical Doctor of the Church, Saint Teresa of Avila, referring to the prayer of quiet: "Thus, when in this state of Quiet, I, who understand hardly anything that I recite in Latin, particularly in the Psalter, have not only been able to understand the text as though it were in Spanish but have even found to my delight that I can penetrate the meaning of the Spanish."[2]

You have chosen to go even further, allowing the music of the chant to enter your innermost selves. Your itinerary has been somewhat similar to that of an atheist, or someone completely indifferent to religion, who happens to stumble upon a church service where Gregorian chant is being sung. He may begin by reacting only to outward impressions, and probably refer to these as theater or folklore. But then, little by little, the neums transform him—the music passes from the outside to the inside. Without his being aware of it, or maybe in spite of himself, the chant casts its wonderful spell on him. You called this stage "interiorization," and held up the *Salve Regina* as an example of it (which reminds me of Marie Noël's[3] story about the maidservant, who, though she did not know the meaning of either *salve* or *regina*, understood the *Salve Regina* perfectly).

From interiorization we go to memorization, which you consider the best method of assimilating the teaching learned from the chant. And indeed, for a long time, chanting was the means by which an entire tradition was handed down, an "oral" tradition, or at least a tradition in which writing was the exception. By learning Gregorian chant by heart, we can rediscover the *cantus obscurior*,[4] the song which, hidden from conscious awareness, is yet at the origin of all vocal music. To hear or sing Gregorian chant is to apprehend the fullness of a language that merely spoken words can never adequately express.

Gregorian chant, then, provides an excellent educational experience, both through the message it presents and the forceful way that message enters the soul.

Gregorian Chant as Prayer

The statement that Gregorian chant is prayer has been repeated so often as to seem commonplace. Nevertheless, it is a profound truth, corresponding fully to the innermost needs of our lives as Christians.

When sung in Gregorian chant, the prayer of the Church is supported by the best music there is for nourishing the soul, music which is also an artistic masterpiece. This music expresses the thoughts and feelings that are at the origin of prayer. Its richness and beauty give rise to prayer, something which the Introit of the First Sunday in Advent defines simply as the lifting up of our soul towards God: "*Ad te levavi animam meam*" (Unto Thee do I lift up my soul).

The chant is characterized by great simplicity. It never resorts to artifice. Dramatic effects are rarely employed, and never for their own sake. There is nothing contrived about

Gregorian chant, despite its elaborate technique. It neither wearies nor stimulates the imagination.

Unlike many of today's compositions, the chant does not permit mediocrity. It is impossible to pray using mediocre means. Instead, as Saint Pius X said, the people of God feel the need to pray through beautiful music.

Beauty which never wearies. And for two reasons. First, Gregorian chant can stand frequent repetition. We can sing the same piece again and again—the simplest *Kyrie,* for example—without tiring. In fact, repetition affords composers a means of expression. It is employed in the easy responsorials or litanies as well as in the more complex pieces.

The second reason we never grow weary of the chant is that the Gregorian repertory offers a prayer that is always new, due to its originality and to the cyclical nature of the liturgy. All this generates a rich variety. No polyphonist has produced anything comparable to it. With its wide assortment of pieces from different periods and places of origin, the chant features great modal and rhythmic diversity. This helps create the impression of something very dynamic—a living, growing internal repertory.

The prayer of Gregorian chant is the public prayer of the Church; it leads to union with God.

That this prayer was used by our ancestors in no way diminishes it in your estimation. On the contrary! You are delighted to know that these very same chants were sung in the past by a multitude of people of good will—some of them authentic, canonized saints—men and women of every era, from different places and various walks of life. This knowledge is a great comfort to you. Gregorian chant invites individuals to receive tradition and, ultimately, to receive Christ. But to do so requires humility and wisdom.

The results obtained are far more effective than anything produced by what is currently advertised as "liturgical creativity" which encourages everyone to reinvent constantly his own liturgical gestures and songs.

You also see Gregorian chant as exceptionally conducive to silence and meditation. Some of you have even said that when you know the repertory well enough, every neum evokes a particular feeling.

I wish to emphasize that all your reflections show the importance you place on attaining a good knowledge of the repertory. Each Gregorian piece is an invitation to prayer. And the entire repertory steeps you and me in a general atmosphere of prayer. It nourishes that prayer day by day. You are not merely "chant-lovers"; Gregorian chant dwells deep within you. It shapes the very depths of your being. At the same time, it bursts from your heart and lifts you, in mind and in heart, towards heaven. Is prayer supposed to be anything else? In the words of Auguste Le Guennant: "Prayer has become music."[5]

Gregorian Chant as a Way of Life

Many of the above thoughts suggest that Gregorian chant is a way of life, as some of you aptly put it. To begin with, the chant helps you to become a more authentic person. It is deeply spiritual because it is profoundly human. You have already experienced to what extent the character and sensitivity of a young person are marked by belonging to a *schola*, how it can touch a soul with a lifelong, maturing influence.

This maturing influence can be felt not only at the human level, but also at the level of Christian life. Nearly all of you speak most clearly about the role of Gregorian chant in your lives as Christians. This, for you, is its most beautiful aspect; the chant is religious music of the highest quality because of its intrinsically liturgical nature. In believing this you refuse to go along with those liturgists who consider music a rather bothersome ornament that certain people insist upon adding to prayer texts. Rather, in your eyes, the chant is an intrinsic element of the liturgy, just as it was for those who composed the chants in former times.

You are unable to conceive of liturgy without the chant which, being of the highest quality, can never be relegated to a secondary or complementary role, or still worse, considered useless. On the contrary, the chant is so entwined with the essence of the liturgical act that viewing it as a mere ornament reduces the liturgy itself to a theatrical act. Hence your penetrating conclusion: Gregorian chant becomes the liturgy!

Gregorian chant leads some Christians to a new life, or rather to a better defined form of the Christian life; it can spark and nourish a priestly vocation, or a calling to the religious life. Actually, all of you, through Gregorian chant, are aware of a pull toward the religious life, understood in the most basic etymological sense of the word "religious." For the chant makes you deepen your *relationship* with God.

To sum up these general thoughts on our lives as human beings and Christians, and on the priestly or religious vocations, we could say that Gregorian chant helps bring unity to the soul, enabling a person to be at one with himself.

But the chant also brings about another type of unity— unity among people. You have yourselves verified this through the bonds of friendship forged in the choirs in which you sing. This same brotherhood exists among the various groups of singers devoted to Gregorian chant in the Church.

In a liturgical assembly, the chant unites all those present. Though you barely touched upon this thought, we should take note of it. For whether we sing it or listen to it, Gregorian chant generates unity—more so, perhaps, than any other type of music.

You have, I know, noted the degree to which Gregorian chant, extended through distance and time, unites people from different countries or from different generations into the same kind of spiritual life. In so doing, it creates a distinct sense of the universal Church and manifests the communion of the saints.

Finally, and self-evidently, Gregorian chant unites us to God. When we speak of our Christian life, we imply that we share in the divine life. Gregorian chant does not simply inculcate in us the feeling or sense of who God is. It actually makes us holy, and enables us to participate in the life of God. And thus, it acts as an authentic means of sanctification.

The chant is not of course one of the sacraments, whose effects are *ex opere operato.*[6] Yet a widely held theological opinion considers the chant to be a "sacramental," operating through the charity of the Church—*ex opere operantis ecclesiae*—that is, producing effects of sanctification stemming from the virtue of the Church that sings her liturgy. Although you did not touch upon this idea, all of you, implicitly or explicitly, believed that participation in divine life was the ultimate goal. One of you divided his reflections into three chapters: (1) Gregorian chant helps us to understand that *listening* is a fundamental aspect of spiritual life; (2) Gregorian chant helps us to experience liturgical prayer; and (3) Gregorian chant helps build the Church. A triple role is thus assigned to the chant: listening, experiencing, edifying.

Perhaps we should touch on the last aspect, understood in its double meaning of bettering others, and building the Church. The chant, as noted, is a source of unity among Catholics, since it enables them to pray together in an atmosphere of beauty. But this beauty also attracts the attention of others, of non-Catholics. We could use this as a starting point to discuss the ecumenical value of Gregorian chant. It is ecumenical both from the horizontal point of view, since it unites people in its beauty, and from the vertical, because it leads us all to God.

Conclusion

And now for your last comments, which can serve as a conclusion.

One of you asked, "Is there any norm other than an aesthetic or poetic one for determining the mood of the musical text of a piece? If it is only a question of aesthetics, what are the criteria to be used? For example, what can we say about the Introit for Easter Sunday, *Resurrexi*, as far as the text and the music are concerned, and the relationship between the two?"

The answer to this question was provided, unknowingly, by another of you. "In the Introit *Resurrexi*, the melody and the modality guide us into the very heart of the mystery of the Blessed Trinity. What is being sung here could never have been merely recited. We are dealing with much more than a simple ornamentation of the words of Christ.[7] As we say these words with the Church, we live and experience them fully in Him."

Thus we can say that when a chant is examined separately, its spiritual significance, which goes beyond the words, rests entirely on criteria of an aesthetic nature.

But the situation is somewhat different when the repertory is considered as a whole, either as a function of the liturgy, or concerning the conditions necessary for its execution. As an element of the liturgy, as we have seen, the Gregorian repertory participates in the spiritual meaning of the entire liturgy.

We still need to say something about the conditions necessary for Gregorian chant to be executed. In this respect, you emphasized the required moral dispositions.

Singing, as you know, implies the willingness to listen: in choir, we need to listen to our neighbors, and we must pay constant and careful attention to the melody itself. Here you stress the need to practice discretion, which presupposes humility.

Listening is the first step on the road to spiritual progress. In this connection, you speak of the Gradual from the Mass for Holy Virgins, *Audi filia* ("Hearken, O daughter"), a text which brings to mind the very first words of the *Rule of Saint Benedict, "Ausculta, o fili"* ("Listen, my son"). You then develop your thought by employing three other key terms in Benedictine spirituality: *taciturnitas* (which does not mean quite the same thing as "taciturnity"), *obœdientia* (obedience), and *humilitas* (humility). *Taciturnitas* is a positive value, implying the *love* of silence. It is necessary in order to perform the chant because we need to listen to inner silence, even while singing. Obedience is also necessary, obedience to the choirmaster of course, but also and more importantly to the melody itself, in order to master its technique and understand its sacred character. As for humility, it implies precisely the willingness to listen, and to be obedient, despite each individual's desire to stand out. Listening obliges us to direct our attention outward, to things other than the self, while our voice, according to Claudel,[8] becomes the instrument of conscience. And here our conscience is engaged in recognizing the identity and qualities of our neighbor, and beyond our neighbor, of our God.

And thus, as you said, God will recognize the accomplishment of his own marvelous works in us. To put it another way, he will be better able to recognize in us the image of His Son.

Let us end by paraphrasing Saint Benedict. If you truly search for God, somewhat like a Benedictine novice, you will end up by reaching, through Gregorian chant, the highest peaks of doctrine and virtue. To quote the last words of the *Rule,* "You will attain the sublime pinnacle of thought and life."[9]

Endnotes

[1] *The Rule of Saint Benedict,* chapter 4: "The instruments of good works" begin with the double precept of Christ concerning love of God and neighbor and the Ten Commandments. They continue with the different exercises and spiritual attitudes of the monastic life, and the various works of charity.

[2] *Complete Works of Saint Teresa,* translated by E. Allison Peers, Vol. I, page 92, Sheed and Ward, London, 1946.

[3] Marie Noël is the pen-name of Marie Rouget, 1883-1968, well-known French poet who frequently visited Solesmes.

[4] The term *cantus obscurior* was first used by Cicero in order to designate the music implicitly contained in the Latin words themselves because of the accents.

[5] August Le Guennant 1881-1972, a church musician who devoted his life to the active promotion of Gregorian chant.

[6] Among the rites of the Catholic Church, theology distinguishes between two categories: (1) the seven "sacraments," which

invariably produce their effects, "ex opere operato," i.e., in virtue of the action itself; these rites were instituted directly by Christ, and are accomplished by Him, with the sacred minister only acting as instrument; (2) "sacramentals," which were instituted by the Church, and which produce their effects "ex opere operantis," i.e., in virtue of the merits and prayers of the Church.

[7] The Easter Sunday Introit *Resurrexi* is drawn from the Ancient Latin version of Psalm 138, verse 18, based on the Septuagint Greek translation of the Bible. It begins with the words "I have risen and am still with thee"; these are attributed by the liturgy to Christ, greeting His Father at the moment of His Resurrection from the dead.

[8] Paul Claudel, 1868-1955, celebrated Catholic poet and playwrite.
[9] *The Rule of Saint Benedict,* chapter 73.

2

Sacred Chant

Having examined your reflections in our first gathering, we will now read some texts which will not only parallel your thoughts, but complete them and provide a framework for your future reflections.

Gregorian Chant

First of all, we should ask: In exactly what sense are we using the term "Gregorian chant"? Without going into detail, we will employ the term here in its broadest sense, despite the drawbacks of such a definition. We will look at every musical genre related to Latin liturgical monody, from the simplest recitatives to the richest melismatic chants, as well as the various historical stages of the repertory; this will include its later outgrowths, that is, certain "prose sequence" compositions and hymns. In addition, we will not distinguish between what is referred to as "Gregorian" chant and the other Latin liturgical repertories—Ambrosian, Mozarabic, and so on.

Obviously, this general explanation will not fit each individual piece perfectly. But no matter; our aim is to find certain common traits.

The broad definition of the term "Gregorian chant" is valid for two reasons, one positive the other negative. The positive reason is that these chants seem to belong to the same family. They look related. This is not an uneducated opinion; it is shared by a good many musicologists. These scholars are apt not to distinguish between the various Latin repertories or the different musical genres of the chant. For them, all Latin liturgical chants belong to one and the same category. I had an example of this recently when I asked various musicologists whether they thought Old Roman chant was more ancient than Gregorian and discovered that they found no difference whatsoever between the two repertories!

The negative reason in favor of our definition is that, in the broadest sense, Gregorian chant has little or nothing in common with other musical forms, such as polyphony or symphonic music. Gregorian chant constitutes a distinct category in the field of religious music. It is even different from other monodic forms—Latin or vernacular, ancient or modern, such as oratorios, hymns, Negro spirituals, and so on.

Our current definition of "Gregorian chant," moreover, corresponds to that of Vatican II, which recognized Gregorian chant as "the chant proper to the Roman liturgy."[1] True, the Council fathers never actually explained what they meant by "Gregorian chant." But they did distinguish it from other types of sacred music, particularly from polyphony. In referring to it, they adopted the accepted use of the term.

But why did they call it the "chant proper to the Roman liturgy," all but saying "*the* chant of the Church"?

Obviously because both canonically and in practice, Gregorian chant was just that at the opening of the Council. And because throughout the centuries, it had been universally sung in the Latin Church. (These historical and geographical factors will be taken up in due course.)

This "chant proper to the Church" is sacred. This aspect of Gregorian chant will be gone into in detail. Here, let us begin by quoting from Pius X's *Motu Proprio* which declares: "Sacred music must possess to the utmost level those characteristics proper to the liturgy—holiness and excellence of form—which in turn spontaneously give birth to the liturgy's other characteristic, universality. . . These qualities exist to a supreme degree in Gregorian chant."[2]

The ideas we are going to discuss concern the spirituality of Gregorian chant. Boiled down: what is it in the chant that gives it its sacred character? The answer, quite simply, is the chant's intrinsic nature and the use to which it has been put.

In the present talk, we hope to show how the chant is sacred in an indirect way, in a way that stems from its assigned role or function. Later we will examine three aspects of the chant—its liturgical, musical, and philosophical traits—in order to show how Gregorian chant's sacred character is derived from its very nature. These characteristics will be the topics of the three following talks.

The Service of God

Gregorian chant is sacred because of its role in the liturgy and divine office. It was made for the temple of God; that is its ultimate destination, its destiny. It plays a purely religious role. Its prime, if not unique objective is to serve as a vehicle for prayer. It always aims, sometimes indirectly, most often directly, at praising the Lord. Although the chant can also contribute to the "consolation and sanctification of the faithful," this is a secondary goal, always closely linked to the chant's primary, God-centered purpose—self-evident to anyone familiar with the repertory. Those who have intimately experienced the atmosphere proper to Gregorian chant become more and more aware of the fact. To illustrate this, we need to examine three aspects of the chant: the chant in history; the chant today; the chant's intrinsic nature.

The Chant in History

Sacred music has existed throughout history, and it has constantly needed to ward off the intrusions—infiltration or invasion—of secular music. We will not seek to deal extensively with this chronic difficulty except to make a few remarks about Gregorian chant.

We could start by probing the chant's origin. Did it spring up spontaneously in the sanctuary, or is it an example of how an originally secular musical language is taken up by the Church?

Historical documents dating back to the first centuries of Christianity show that anything that evoked the pagan world and its songs was categorically excluded from Christian basilicas. The cantillation of the sacred texts of Scripture in the Church (the earliest form of Christian liturgical chant) belongs to an entirely different aesthetic world; its most likely ancestor would be the sacred music of synagogues.

Later, when the schola wrote its own more specialized and elaborate repertory—for example, the Gradual-Responsories of the Mass and the long Responsories of the divine office—there is no evidence of any borrowing from secular music. On the contrary, research reveals an internal development, an evolution from the simpler forms of cantillation to more complex pieces. Of course, much still needs to be clarified, primarily the type of musical formation received by the expert cantors who produced the schola repertory.

History shows that from the ninth century on, Western music grew out of Gregorian chant. Does this mean that Gregorian chant was sometimes used in a profane and secular way?

Not at all. Although medieval music does owe a great deal to Gregorian chant, it hardly ever borrows from it directly. (There are, of course, exceptions like the *Office of Fools*, devised as a musical joke by young clerics or altar boys.) The secular music of the Middle Ages did indeed derive from Gregorian chant, but it took on its own shape and character. It made use of Gregorian formulas and tenors, but transformed them radically, totally restructuring them. In the realm of modality, it opted in favor of newer sonorities, thus ushering in modern tonality.

Nor can the use of chant tenors by sixteenth-century polyphony, and the use of Gregorian motifs by more recent composers like Debussy or Dubosq, be construed as secularization—much less symphonic and operatic music which is separated by a great gulf from Gregorian chant. As for the "antimusic" in vogue today, suffice to say that, by contrast, we can all the better appreciate the sacred character of chant.

The Chant's Sacred Character Today

Is Gregorian chant currently in danger of being sung in a profane way, through contempt—or just plain ignorance—of its religious character? Is it being absorbed into the domain of secular "culture"?

With regard to the first question, a risk is clearly involved. We live in a world that respects absolutely nothing. Still, we can take comfort in the thought that Gregorian chant is so foreign to some that they simply ignore it, or are indifferent to it. For others, of course, it evokes a nostalgia for the unknown and exerts the mysterious attraction of a lost paradise. True, on very rare occasions rock music recordings or motion picture soundtracks have employed bits of Gregorian chant in a profane and almost blasphemous way. But several young people who have visited Solesmes claim that this was how they first became aware of the chant, a discovery that ultimately led some of them to an authentic interest in the liturgy—and eventually to conversion.

As far as Gregorian chant in the cultural domain is concerned, its inclusion in the study programs of conservatories and institutes of musicology is in no way a bad thing. Its occasional performance in concerts, and even, (as this present edition goes to press) its astounding success in Spain on the top ten list of "golden oldies" can help to arouse public interest, somewhat compensating for the unfair discrimination against Gregorian chant in certain clerical circles. Any music worthy of the name can inspire enthusiasm no matter where it is heard. "Any piece of music can lay a claim to being 'sacred,' if it is shown to be a means of broadening the mind, and not solely a source of pleasure."[3] These two remarks apply in a special way to Gregorian chant which carries within itself and seeks to communicate so deep a spiritual message.

The religious and cultural aspects of Gregorian chant are actually inseparable. The human element cannot be perceived without the divine, and vice versa. This was what a Japanese gentleman meant when he said, "This music is sacred and it belongs to the heritage of all humankind." He perceived it as a means of sharpening his own human and Japanese identity. The members of the group he directs, nearly all Buddhists, believe that Gregorian chant is the most profoundly religious music in existence, and they practice it as such.

Sacred in Its Very Essence

These reflections, as well as a rapid glance at the history of Gregorian chant, lead to the following statement: Gregorian chant is sacred by its very nature.

And because Gregorian chant is sacred, it is fitting and logical that from the very beginning it should have been set apart exclusively for divine use. We thus come full circle: the underlying essence of the chant confirms the historical facts.

To end, let us quote Simone Weil: "It is quite conceivable that someone who is a passionate music lover might at the same time be evil or corrupt as a person. But I would find it hard to believe that such a thing could be true of anyone who has a thirst for Gregorian chant."[4]

Endnotes

[1] *Constitution on the Sacred Liturgy,* art. 116.
[2] Pope Pius X, *Motu Proprio* of November 22, 1903, nos. 2 and 3, cf. Robert F. Hayburn, *Papal Legislation on Sacred Music,* p. 224. Liturgical press Collegeville, 1979
[3] (See Bibliography), J. Porte, *Encyclopédie des musiques sacrées,* op.cit., p.18.
[4] Simone Weil, *La Pesanteur et la Grâce,* Paris, Plon, 1948, p. 174.

3

Liturgical Chant

Gregorian chant is sacred because its character is essentially liturgical. In reference to this, we need to examine two very different problems:

1. The relationship between Gregorian chant and the "sacred text," a term which is applied here not only to Holy Scripture but also to various ecclesiastical compositions such as the Collects.

2. How Gregorian chant participates in the specific characteristics that define the liturgy.

Other aspects of the chant—the way it shares in the spiritual, contemplative, and sanctifying energies of the liturgy, of which it is an element—will be taken up in the last talk.

Gregorian Chant and the Sacred Text

The language of Gregorian chant is necessarily Latin. (The occasional Hebrew or Greek words, like "Alleluia" or "Kyrie eleison," were assimilated into liturgical Latin.) This is not the moment to take up in detail the controversy over the use of a sacred language. The reasons for using Latin are quite clear to those who have studied Gregorian chant spirituality. Cardinal G. M. Garronne put the case well: "It escapes the changes that are an inevitable part of the constant evolution of any modern language. It is an integral part of that marvel of religious art that is Gregorian chant. It taps our entire past history and joins our prayers with the very same prayers of our forefathers."[1]

All sacred languages tend to create a certain holy or "hieratic" atmosphere. They build a wall between the sacred and the secular, between the words of prayer and the common speech of everyday life. A sacred language is not meant to be immediately intelligible to just anyone. As an Englishwoman once wrote to me: "When conversing with God, I wouldn't care to employ the same expressions I use when talking to my butcher."

With this as background, we can look at the ingenious and highly artistic way, amply revealed by musical analysis, in which the Gregorian composers set the Latin words and phrases to music. In polyphonic anthems, by contrast, the music is so rich that it tends to eclipse the Latin text, drawing attention to the music rather than to the words or thought. At its best, polyphony serves to amplify a feeling or prolong a meditation. The same is true of orchestral music.

Rev. Fr. A. D. Sertillanges, the well-known Dominican theologian, used to say: "Religious chant is born from increasing slightly the emphasis given the words pro-nounced during prayer."[2] This is particularly true of Gregorian chant, especially in the simple antiphons and some of the hymns. And it was amply illustrated by Canon Jean

Jeanneteau,[3] who declaimed the *Lauda Sion* ("O Zion, praise thy Savior") with increasing emphasis, until he ended with the sequence's traditional, well-known melody.

Thus, the chant is not merely a decorative garment, haphazardly tacked on to the text for better or for worse. Unfortunately, a good many liturgists appear utterly incapable of comprehending this fact.

Musicians, on the other hand, admire the harmony that exists between chant and word throughout the Gregorian repertory, even in the most ornate melodies. The reason is quite simple—word and music are not two separate entities but one and the same reality. Rev. Fr. J. Y. Hameline, an apt pupil of Canon Jean Jeanneteau, put it well. In brief: "It is not a question of adding music to the words, nor even of setting words to music . . . Instead, it is a question of making the words bring forth the music they already contain . . . We do not have the text on the one hand . . . and the melody on the other . . . but rather a unique monody . . . in which the melody sings the words correctly, precisely because these words gave the music its initial motion. The words, in turn, support the melody and cause it to sing because of the melody's role, which is to transfigure the text's meaning, rhythm, and elemental sonority."[4]

Earlier, Pope Leo XIII had given his own definition of the harmonious relationship between melody and word: "In truth, the Gregorian melodies were composed with much prudence and wisdom, in order to elucidate the meaning of the words. There resides within them a great strength and a wonderful sweetness mixed with gravity, all of which readily stirs up religious feelings in the soul, and nourishes beneficial thoughts just when they are needed. . . ."[5]

Gregorian Chant and the Specific Characteristics of the Liturgy

Prosper Guéranger (writing as a young secular priest, before becoming a monk and the first abbot of Solesmes), tried to define the liturgy by enumerating the following "notes," as he put it, or distinguishing qualities, namely: antiquity, universality, authority, and unction.[6] In current parlance we would probably call them permanence, catholicity, authenticity, and devotion. But let us use Dom Guéranger's terminology. Our goal is to examine whether these four traits, which were applied to define the liturgy, can also be applied to Gregorian chant. Remember that the first two correspond exactly to the well-known characteristics advanced by St. Vincent of Lérins in A.D. 434, to distinguish between authentic Christian dogma and the teachings of heretics: *quod ubique semper* (what the Church has taught always and everywhere).[7]

Antiquity

Here we encounter a difficulty. The term "antiquity" applies to institutions and documents dating from the primitive Church or from the Patristic era, which in Western Christendom is generally thought to end before the middle of the seventh century, But, as we shall soon see, the ornate Gregorian melodies in their present, classical form did not come into being until the end of the eighth century. Therefore, certain critics have argued that Gregorian chant has no real claim to antiquity.

Reasoning of this kind fails to take into account the pro-found unity existing in the Gregorian repertory between elements that come from different historical periods, and which were faithfully conserved and handed down by oral tradition, and the remarkably conservative manner in which medieval musicians utilized their sources when devising new melodies.

Most of the prayer recitatives or "cantillations" used in Gregorian chant really do date from antiquity, reaching back to the very first centuries of the Church. The more recent, ornate melodies give the impression of flowing in a direct and continuous line from this primitive source. Introduced for the professional singers of the schola, they were carefully built on the more primitive elements. Their diversification and evolution have remained faithful to the same basic principles. The chant's homogenous development is thus unmistakable, and the entire repertory gives the impression of being "one and the same family."

Of course, other, more ancient repertories of ornate Latin chants did exist, all of them apparently having much stronger claims to "antiquity." But these can be divided into two categories—those that were sober and sparing in their methods (Beneventine and "Old Roman"), and those that were rich and elaborate (Milanese, Gallican, and Hispanic). Gregorian chant came into being as the result of the encounter between repertories from these two families. It appears to have been created shortly after the liturgy used in Rome was imported by imperial decree into the Carolingian Empire, around 750 A.D., along with the melodies of the "Old Roman chant." In short order, these melodies were radically transformed by the Frankish cantors who used local, "Gallican" styles of ornamentation. Thus, Gregorian chant represents a vast synthesis and can be referred to as the "classic" chant form of antiquity.

We know, of course, that the chant survived over subsequent centuries, despite the evolution and vicissitudes of musical taste. Long after it had been totally disfigured and distorted, in the late Middle Ages and Renaissance, it managed to retain part of its individual character. Even as late as the seventeenth and eighteenth centuries, "plain chant" contrasted with "music"; "singing in plain chant" contrasted with just plain "singing." In its very decadence, the chant continued to exhibit those characteristics of medieval art which Solange Corbin defined as detachment of self, dedication to duty, and respect for tradition. It eschewed independence of spirit, novelty, self-centeredness, and individualism.[8]

Details of this could be debated at length, but the basic idea holds true. Canon Jean Beilliard, for one, felt that the decline of Gregorian chant went hand in hand with man's declining awareness of and appreciation for God, Jesus Christ, and the Church. He demonstrated this decline by pointing to what ensued—the anthropocentric polyphony of the Renaissance; the Protestant chorale; the new music and new texts which sprang from seventeenth- and eighteenth-century rationalism; and finally the ousting of God completely, which was the triumph of materialism.[9] And since Canon Beilliard was speaking in the midst of the liturgical movement of the 1950s, he knew nothing of the unfortunate innovations that were to crop up in the post-Vatican II era. But all this aside, if today's better understanding of the Gregorian repertory, and therefore of its execution, were to bring about a new Golden Age of Gregorian chant, it would affirm more than ever the antiquity of the chant.

Last of all, a discussion of Gregorian chant's antiquity

brings to mind another, related trait—its permanence. Concerning this, we can refer to Jacques Chailley, the well-known music history expert, who sees Gregorian chant as exemplifying the permanent aspects of music as opposed to its transitory, or "fleeting" aspects.

Universality

As the official liturgical song of the Latin Church, Gregorian chant necessarily shares in the Church's universal character.

The existence of various other medieval Latin chant repertories in no way contradicts this universality. To begin with, all the Latin repertories are branches of the same trunk, following similar patterns of evolution from simple cantillation to more ornate melodies. The more ancient pre-Gregorian or non-Gregorian forms characterized particular regions and most of them were finally supplanted altogether by the Gregorian repertory. But it would be quite unfair to point to this as an instance of the way in which local diversities are sometimes sacrificed in the interests of uniformity and centralization. Although it is true that Gregorian chant was created as part of the effort to extend the unity of the Roman liturgy to the Frankish Empire, the final result was an admirable synthesis in which the imported "Old Roman" melodies were totally transfigured by the local, Gallican musical practices. The new, revitalized repertory proved to be the apogee of the Latin chant tradition and its rapid triumph everywhere was due almost exclusively to the strength of its own merits.

The most eloquent proof of Gregorian chant's universal character is the extraordinary fidelity of its manuscript tradition. The chant was at first transmitted orally, but by the end of the ninth century it was being written on manuscripts with neums—musical notation without lines. Over a period of several centuries it was copied and recopied, and its manuscripts spread to all corners of Christian Europe—from Ireland to Sicily, and from Spain to Poland. Astoundingly, although the output of these manuscripts was massive, there were very few mistakes and practically no variants of any major import. This fundamental unanimity demonstrates how faithfully our ancestors conserved the tradition. It also, of course, proves the extent to which Gregorian chant entered into the cultural fabric of the various European nations.

More recently, Gregorian chant has spread beyond the boundaries of Western and Central Europe, thus confirming that its universality is not *de facto* but an inherent characteristic. Africans, for example, can assimilate it perfectly. People from the Far East are also sensitive to its appeal; they eagerly listen to it, study it, and even practice it, although it belongs to a musical ethos quite different from their own.

Gregorian chant's universality contrasts sharply with the particularity of other musical forms, which tend to have a temporary as well as a local life. Such was the case with the polyphonic compositions of the sixteenth century that sprang from Spain, Flanders, Italy, and elsewhere, and the eighteenth-century hymns from places such as France and Germany, beautiful though they all may have been.

Another important aspect of Gregorian chant is its role in the ecumenical movement. The chant is the common heritage of Western Christendom, predating by centuries the Reformation rupture. With respect to the Greek Church, it reigned in a period when diverse but complementary liturgical and spiritual traditions coexisted in an undivided Church. Today, Gregorian chant continues to be practiced by several Christian confessions. On a broader scale, it is the musical form most closely related to the ancient Eastern and Jewish models, as well as other exotic musical styles. It forms a part of the universal musical heritage of humanity.

Authority

The patronage of Gregorian chant was for a long time popularly attributed to Saint Gregory the Great. But since this assertion is almost certainly fictitious or legendary, it cannot serve as an argument for the chant's authenticity.[10]

In truth, it was only much later that Popes began to place Gregorian chant under their direct patronage. Papal documents giving explicit approbation date no earlier than the nineteenth century, with the exception, perhaps, of one text that goes back to Benedict XIV in 1749.[11] But it is equally true that long before this, Gregorian chant had *implicit* papal approval. In the thirteenth century, for example, it became the official chant of the Roman curia, thanks to the influence of the Franciscans. In 1277, Nicholas III replaced the books of the primitive Old Roman chant, which up until then had been used in the basilicas of the Eternal City, with the books of the Franciscans who used the Gregorian version.[12]

It would be equally vain to search for early episcopal documents to support the thesis that Gregorian chant was the favored musical expression of the Church. These do not exist, for the excellent reason that, for many centuries, the need for such legislation never occurred to anyone, since the privileged place of Gregorian chant was implicitly understood. The Church was content simply to sing the chant. She faithfully maintained the heritage of past generations while allowing it to develop creatively.

"Government-imposed" music was almost unheard of— except, as noted, when Pepin the Short and Charlemagne brought the Old Roman chant to their empire. But once arrived in the Frankish Empire it immediately underwent radical change and became our classical Gregorian chant form.

The true authority of Gregorian chant rests not on rubrics or legislative decrees, but rather on the *consensus populi* (the common assent of the people of God) and the *sensus ecclesiae* (the supernatural sense of discernment of the Church). Led by their priests and bishops, the faithful everywhere have always sung Gregorian chant. It draws its authority from a vast number of enthusiastic Catholic Christians. Throughout the ages, it has been the musical language of the liturgy in the Western Church. The authority of Gregorian chant is based on tradition.

The enduring *de facto* authority of the Gregorian repertory is reinforced by another characteristic that it holds in common with the liturgy as a whole—a quality which Dom Guéranger called "unction." But before proceeding any further we should note the extent to which the four distinguishing qualities of the chant—antiquity, universality, authority, and unction—are linked; they are but four aspects of the same reality, the same perfection.

Unction

Unction is defined by the *Oxford Dictionary* as "a fervent or sympathetic quality in words or tone, caused by or causing deep religious feeling." Dom Guéranger applied the term to the liturgy in general, and thought of it as linked to the spirit of godliness. "It is," he said, "a quality that must be *felt*; but it cannot be *defined*."[13] Its principal author is the Holy Spirit, the Spirit of Divine Love. In the liturgy, it evokes holiness, order, and peace, the opposite of dryness and sterility. Among its secondary origins, Dom Guéranger mentions the holiness and universality of the Church, and the work of the saints. He emphasizes the intimate bond between unction in the liturgy and the spirit of prayer. Unction makes it easier to enter into an attitude of prayer and love. To further his point, Dom Guéranger would point to the dry atmosphere of the "dogmatic" or didactic Neo-Gallican liturgies of his day. They contrasted sharply with the richness and freedom of the authentic Roman liturgy that he sought so hard to restore.

Unction, or fervor, characterizes not only the liturgy in general but also, in a most particular way, the sacred chant. On several occasions, Saint Paul recommended that we offer, from the heart, hymns, spiritual songs, and prayers of thanksgiving for the fullness of the word of Christ and the Holy Spirit. "Let the word of Christ dwell within you richly, teach and admonish one another in all wisdom, and sing psalms and hymns and spiritual songs with thankfulness in your hearts to God. And whatever you do in word or in deed, do everything in the name of the Lord Jesus, giving thanks to God the Father through him." (Col 3:16-17)

"Be filled with the Spirit, addressing one another in psalms and hymns and spiritual songs, singing and making melody to the Lord with all your heart, always and for everything giving thanks in the name of our Lord Jesus Christ to God the Father." (Eph 5:18-20)

"The Spirit himself intercedes for us with sighs too deep for words." (Rom 8:26)

Unction, or fervor, describes the atmosphere which all authentic religious music seeks to create. Those who have experienced Gregorian chant know how magnificently it achieves this goal. Better than any other musical form, it successfully imparts the fullness of meaning in the words of the Latin liturgy; it transmits a spiritual message from age to age.

Endnotes

[1] Cardinal G. M. Garrone, "For or Against Latin," *Semaine Catholique de Toulouse*, January 17, 1965, reprinted in *Documentation Catholique*, t. LXII, 47th year, February 7, 1965.

[2] (See Bibliography): Sertillanges, op.cit., p. 7

[3] Canon Jean Jeanneteau, 1908-1992, an expert both in the field of electronics and in Gregorian chant.

[4] (See Bibliography): Hameline, op. cit., p. 34-35.

[5] The papal Brief *Nos Quidem*, letter of May 17, 1901, addressed to Dom Delatte, abbot of Solesmes, on the restoration of Gregorian chant. Cf. *Revue grégorienne* 6, 1921, p. 46.

[6] Fr. Prosper Guéranger, "Considérations sur la liturgie," in *Mélanges de liturgie, d'histoire et de théologie*, Solesmes, 1887.

[7] Vincent of Lérins, *Commonitorium*, ch. 2, Patrologia latina, t. 50, col. 640.

[8] (See Bibliography): Corbin, op. cit., pp. 37-40.

[9] (See Bibliography): Canon J. Beilliard, op. cit., p.137, ss.

[10] Among the principal sources of this legend are the *"Gregorius Praesul,"* a short, versified preface found at the beginning of certain ancient manuscripts of the Mass Antiphonary, and the quaint trope *Sanctus Gregorius*, which is often given as a musical introduction to the Introit antiphon of the First Sunday in Advent. Both these documents depict St. Gregory as the author of the particular book

in which they are found, and not of the entire Gregorian chant repertory. In any event, the historical value of this evidence is doubtful.

[11] Benedict XIV, "Annus qui," February 19, 1749, printed in *Les enseignements pontificaux: la liturgie,* Solesmes, 1956, p. 38.

[12] Raoul de Rivo, *De canonum observantia,* XXII; ed. Mohlberg, p. 128.

[13] Fr. Prosper Guéranger—*Memorial catholique,* July 31, 1830, p. 241.

4

The Musical Aspect of Gregorian Chant

Gregorian chant is sacred by virtue of its technical aspects. As in all art forms, a particular set of aesthetic values issue from technical considerations. These, in turn, elicit emotions that influence our subjective judgment concerning the artistic worth of the chant, and its spiritual significance.

Let us examine two technical aspects of Gregorian chant— an objective and a more subjective aspect: (1) the way the technique serves spirituality; and (2) the transition from the technical to subjective impressions.

Our goal is to make a few simple reflections, not to examine systematically the structure of Gregorian chant or its aesthetics.

How the Technical Characteristics Serve Spirituality

Of the multitude of studies that seek to define the musical structure of Gregorian chant, the ones that interest us here are those that consider the effect of the chant's structure on the soul, and its value as prayer. (Dom Joseph Gajard, the former choirmaster of Solesmes, frequently took up this theme. So did his successor, Dom Jean Claire, using a somewhat different approach.)[1]

Let us consider three matters: (1) the nature of Gregorian chant; (2) its language; and (3) its construction.

The Nature of Gregorian Chant

To state the obvious, the essential, fundamental characteristic of Gregorian chant is its pure monophony. Whether the melody is syllabic, ornate, or melismatic, the style always remains linear. Gregorian chant is totally melodic because it excludes any and all concomitant sounds. The relationship between notes is strictly successive. More than any other type of music—and better, perhaps, than any other monophonic musical form—it seems to be aiming at something, or driving towards something. In its progression, it never pauses to savor the "present moment" (in contrast to vertical types of music).

What Gregorian monody is incessantly driving toward is, in the final analysis, the subject of the song. In a secular comparison, French popular songs, for example, are almost invariably about love ("amour" which is rhymed—always— with "toujours"). But Gregorian chants are about the Lord God, His attributes, His grace.

Another aspect of its monophonic nature is that Gregorian chant can be sung by only one person. The chant does not require many performers as is the case in polyphony or orchestral works. Thus each individual is placed directly before God; when singing the chant, a person is automatically placed in a relationship that is of a higher level than anything he can attain with his fellow human beings.

This is not to say that other forms of music, polyphonic and even orchestral, are not religious. (Even the orchestral music of someone like Wagner has a powerful, religious dimension). Nor do we wish entirely to exclude the social aspect of Gregorian chant. It is social, but in the same way that the Church is a society. It totally refuses to play upon our gregarious instincts and never elicits a purely human fellowship. That is, although it establishes a profound sense of unity among cantors and listeners, this unity is not its primary function or effect. For the union it establishes among the faithful seems to flow from the communion it has already established between each individual and the Creator.

The Language of Gregorian Chant

Experts, looking at the chant from an exclusively technical point of view, would probably talk about Pythagorean music as opposed to harmonic music, or about absolute diatonism[2] (although some might spot certain enharmonic nuances there).[3] They emphasize the exclusion of such things as the leading tone, modality (in the sense of the classical Greek modes), and the possibility of modulation.

The musical character of Gregorian chant creates an impression very different from the one produced by what we refer to as "modern music." It makes us feel as if we have been transported to a faraway place, somewhere in the distant past. But does this sufficiently explain its deeply religious character? Archaism and hieraticism tend to go hand in hand. But what is archaic today was novelty in its time.

Did Gregorian chant borrow elements from Greek music? It is difficult to say, since we have almost no concrete idea of what Greek music was like. But what we do know seems to indicate that theoreticians did not begin to define the Gregorian modes in terms of Greek modality until the ninth century, long after the Gregorian repertory had been completely formed. Furthermore, their theories were based upon an inaccurate understanding of Greek modality.

And thus it seems that Gregorian chant is, in fact, a unique musical language; it is *sui generis*. This leaves open, of course, the possibility that ethno-musicologists can establish points of contact between the chant and other forms of music.

The musical language of Gregorian chant stands out through its simplicity and diversity. Without going into the structure of the different modes, we can perceive the character of each of them, subjectively to be sure, but always attuned to the deepest feelings of the soul. We can, that is, go along with Dom Gajard when he speaks about the peaceful character of the *re* mode, the joyous spirit of the *mi,* the freshness of the *fa,* or the enthusiasm of the *sol.*[4]

The Construction of Gregorian Pieces

Dom Joseph Pothier, an early pioneer of the Solesmes chant restoration, attempted to demonstrate that Gregorian chant is an art form by emphasizing several of its traits: its architectural purity, its supple rhythm, and its free yet firm character. He also spoke of its naturalness and versatility, qualities that spurn all that is artificial.[5] Dom André Mocquereau thought along similar lines when he sought to define "Gregorian Art, its goal, its processes, and its character."[6]

Dom Gajard took up the same theme on numerous occasions.[7]

He spoke of the chant's free verbal rhythm and stressed these related points: the indivisibility of the simple time unit, the variety of groupings in larger compound units, and the lack of a strong beat or pulse. Although his definitions were propounded as a contrast to modern music, they also respond to some rhythmic theories. Although we have no time here to review his refutations of these mensuralist theories, the manuscripts provide all the evidence we need to show the extreme freedom of Gregorian rhythm and its diverse finer points of execution.

If we reflect on how serene, noble, light, and mellow the chant can be, we must also note its firmness and rigor, and even, at times, its passionate flame. The structure of the chant is never insipid. Dramatic effects are present, although they are never used as ends in themselves. Thus people have spoken of Gregorian chant's reserve, its chastity, and its poverty—of its being stripped to the barest essentials.[8] Others stress the simplicity of its means, as compared, for example, with orchestral works. They note the limpid way in which the melodies flow, the wonderfully transparent structure. Gregorian phrases really do give the impression of obtaining the maximum effect with the minimum of means, and this would seem to be a mark of true perfection. The Gregorian repertory, moreover, can adapt to the different functions called for in liturgical chant (readings, prayers, antiphons, responsorials, etc.), and to the various categories of singers.

But far more remarkable than any of these individual qualities is the way they all work together. Modality, melodic range, rhythm, and inner drive combine to give the text its full expressive value. This skillful combination can be seen in the "types," that is, in the stereotyped melodies that can adjust to a series of different texts. But it becomes even more evident in the structure of the more original compositions, of the melodies created for a single text—especially many of the shorter pieces, which are often masterpieces in this respect.

In the final analysis, Gregorian chant is praiseworthy for its beauty, understood in both its aesthetic and religious sense. The rigorous "equality" of its rhythm caused Bruno Stäblein to speak of its detachment, which contrasts with the agitation created by the rhythm in contemporary music.[9] The chant is like the icon or the "image of another, supernatural world." Many emphasize the peace that emanates from Gregorian melody, and some have gone so far as to advocate it as a form of therapy.[10] Listeners need no musical analysis to alert them to its free technique which instills a sense of spiritual freedom in their hearts.

These reflections lead to the second part of this talk—the subjective impressions produced by Gregorian chant.

Transition from Technical Aspects to Subjective Impressions

It is difficult to describe Gregorian chant according to the subjective impressions it creates. Not that there is a lack of material on the subject; on the contrary, altogether too much has been written! But, too often, writers have been satisfied with vague impressions, insufficiently precise in form and content, and usually without reference to musical technique. Thus, while we can find authors who, for example, speak of "the prayer of Gregorian chant," they usually fail to explain clearly why and in what sense Gregorian chant really is a prayer.

In order to help us wade through the mass of literature on the subject, perhaps we should establish the following three points:

—Gregorian chant is beautiful.
—Gregorian chant transports us into another world.
—The "universe of Gregorian chant" is the universe of prayer.

Beauty

Beauty is without doubt the most commonly perceived quality of Gregorian chant, even though some listeners, probably the majority, could not explain *why* they find it beautiful. Men and women from every walk of life, including the simplest, hear in the chant something which differs sharply from what they call "cheap music." As witness, recall the wide success of "Gregorian chant Masses," or of Gregorian chant records and cassettes, even though all of them do not achieve the same level of perfection. It is useless to try to explain away this success as some kind of passing fad or as the manifestation of a partisan spirit among Christians with conservative leanings. These factors have little or nothing to do with the matter. The simple truth is that when people are exposed to Gregorian chant, they react to a beauty which is capable of affecting even children.

This beauty is readily accessible. The reason is simplicity—one of Gregorian chant's main characteristics. Thus it is easy to understand this music, or more accurately, to discern its message. Auguste Le Guennant spoke of a "spirituality that is capable of being easily and directly assimilated."[11] The Latin text is not a barrier to understanding, provided one is sensitive to what the music expresses. It is a little like the reaction of a young Cambodian who visited Solesmes: "Gregorian chant is not meant to be sung, but rather to be listened to, because it is a language of its own."

Beauty, immediately perceived, ensures the transmission of a message.

The World of the Sacred

A second reflection commonly made about Gregorian chant might be worded thus: "It transports you into a different world." Two ideas lie behind this assertion.

First, our statement underlines a radical difference between Gregorian chant and all other musical languages or fields. In a vague but perfectly adequate manner, it points out the distance separating the chant from contemporary music. This distance may be due to the chant's archaic character, which comes through in its modality, rhythm, and so on. But there is a good deal more to it than that. Despite its archaic nature, the chant does not strike us as foreign. On the contrary, we feel a profound affinity for it. The best way to express it, then, would be to say that Gregorian chant creates a separation—a separation from all that is profane, secular, and worldly. At the same time, however, the chant is a source of unity. This is our second idea, which we will explore in due course.

A serious analysis of the most common subjective reactions to Gregorian chant brings us to the notion of the chant as a *religious* or, more exactly, a *sacred* art form. (According to Stanislas Fumet, the term "religious" indicates that we are speaking to God; the term "sacred" implies that God is speaking to us.")[12]

In enumerating the elements that contribute to the sacred character of Gregorian chant, we should note, along with Stanislas Fumet, that sensitivity overrides sentimentality. And sensitivity leads to contemplation. Note as well that freedom is not license: preexisting, conventional forms impose a pattern which is automatically conducive to the elevation of souls. (Stravinsky developed this idea when he discussed his *Oedipus*.)[13]

One last corollary. Since, as we have said, Gregorian chant is a song of praise, it is necessarily disinterested. There is nothing commercial about it; it leads us away from a world in which money is all too often the moving force and goal of life.

Prayer

The sacred universe into which Gregorian chant introduces us is the world of prayer—or, if you prefer, of union with God, which is the ultimate goal or aim of prayer. The many reasons for this could be summarized in three characteristics of the chant: spontaneity, depth, and truth.

The chant's spontaneity derives from the almost undefinable aura of purity which it has about it—purity of technique, expression, and intent. Other nuances are simplicity, dignity, and discretion. But these can all be summed up by a single word: humility.

The chant's depth comes from its calm or gravity, which produces serenity and balance. These in turn give rise to an atmosphere filled with gentleness, strength, and peace. It has often been said that Gregorian chant removes us from our ordinary surroundings, makes us lose our bearings, sets us apart. Dom Gajard described it as an "interiorizing" effect; we enter into ourselves, not for any introspective self-analysis, but in order to rediscover the One Who dwells within us.

Even more: Dom Gajard, along with people like the Dominican, Dom Delalande, maintains that Gregorian chant is in fact a sacramental.[14] This amounts to saying that the chant is the truest and most authentic form of sacred music. "To glorify the divine, and not man" is the aim of all sacred music. Gregorian chant perfectly attains this goal. It can in all honesty be said of the chant that "the sounds, rising from silence, must necessarily return to silence."[15] Gregorian chant is perfectly true to the means it employs, excluding as it does all that is artificial. It is true to its ultimate goal, as well, because it strives not only to create a mood but to establish an authentic *communion*.

Let us close these reflections on the connection between technique and the spirituality of Gregorian chant by once again quoting Simone Weil, who denounces the abusive pretensions of modern science, ever since the Renaissance, for its tendency to turn people away from their faith instead of confirming them in that faith.

"If science," she says, "were once again to become faithful to its origin and destiny, rigor in the field of mathematics would contribute to the advance of charity, just as musical technique in the Gregorian melodies works towards the advance of charity. There is a higher degree of musical technique in Gregorian chant than even in Bach or Mozart. Gregorian chant is simultaneously pure technique and pure love, just as any great art form should be."[16]

Endnotes

[1] Dom Joseph Gajard, *La valeur artistique,* op. cit. Dom Jean Claire, "La structure du chant grégorien," *Le Chant Choral,* 1976, no. 10-11. p. 20-29.

[2] (See Bibliography): M. Emmanuel, op. cit., p.66.

[3] In his *Dictionnaire Pratique et Historique de la Musique,* Paris, Colin, 1926, Michael Brenet makes the following remark: "Enharmonics . . . were preserved for a long time in Gregorian chant." Several writers have since agreed, but other musicologists prefer to look for a pentatonic origin of the chant.

[4] (See Bibliography): Dom J. Gajard, *La Valeur Artistique et Religieuse du Chant Grégorien.* This study sums up the author's views on the subject.

It would be interesting to make a study of the various opinions on this topic given by authors, or found in the manuscripts. Of particular interest are the two column capitals in the sanctuary of Cluny III, which represent the eight modes. See "die Darstellung der Tone an den Kapitellen der Abeikirche zu Cluny" (1929), recently reprinted in *De Scientia Musicae Studia et Orationes,* Bern, 1967, pp. 113-151.

[5] Dom Joseph Pothier, "Gregorian Chant as an Art-Form," speech delivered at the Gregorian Congress in Rome on April 9, 1904, and published by the *Rassegna Gregoriana,* 1904, pp. 4, 5.

[6] Dom André Mocquereau, at a conference given at the Catholic Institute of Paris, March 14, 1894, published at Solesmes, 1896.

[7] (See Bibliography) Dom Joseph Gajard, op. cit.

[8] Delalande, op. cit., applies to Gregorian chant the three religious vows.

[9] B. Stäblein, *Encyclopédie des musiques sacrées,* vol. II, p. 80.

[10] See, among contemporary authorities, Dr. Alfred Tomatis. Prior to him, A.E.M. Gréty and others (cf. A. Colling, op.cit., pp. 170-176) had already recognized the therapeutic effects of music.

[11] Op. cit., A. Le Guennant, p. 21.

[12] Op. cit., S. Fumet, p. 377.

[13] Igor Stravinsky, *Chronicles of My Life,* Paris, Denoël-Gonthier, 1935, vol. 2, p. 94.

[14] In this present work see above, Chapter I, note 6 (see page 16). Cf. Gajard, "L'expression dans le chant grégorien," p. 50; Delalande, op. cit., p. 182, does not use the word "sacramental," but he speaks of the way in which Gregorian chant highlights the theological contents of the liturgy.

[15] Op. cit., J. Porte, p. 15.

[16] Simone Weil, *Intuitions Prè-Chrètiennes,* Paris, 1951, "La Colombe," Editions du Vieux Colombier, p. 134

5

The Philosophical Dimension of Gregorian Chant

The sacred character of Gregorian chant is also apparent at the philosophical level. Thus, in this third part of our study, we will examine Gregorian chant spirituality from a philosophical point of view—which leads ultimately to theology. In our search, we will penetrate beyond the simple fact that the chant is used in church; we will go beyond its liturgical value and its technical elements in order to reach the depths of its nature.

And here we face a double or even triple difficulty. First, much of what we say about Gregorian chant is true of all authentically good music; in consequence, we will be dealing with a question of degree, or of relative perfection. Second, our philosophical inquiry runs the risk of becoming overly precise. And finally, the subject in itself is difficult to discuss.

The ideal procedure, perhaps, would be to follow a methodical itinerary; we would travel the road from sensory impressions to union with God, en route passing systematically through psychology, ethics, metaphysics, and at the summit, theology. A number of distinguished Dominicans, like A. D. Sertillanges and D. M. Delalande, have taken a certain road. We prefer the path of Guillaume de Saint Thierry, who suggested the following itinerary: (1) *corpus,* (2) *anima,* and (3) *animus* or *spiritus;* in other words, he passed from considering man as animal, to man as rational being, and finally to man as a spiritual being who ultimately achieves oneness in spirit with God. Pascal himself would have embraced this manner of procedure.

But whichever approach we follow, it will be apparent at every stage that music, and especially Gregorian chant, leads us beyond ourselves. It is fundamentally the connection between two stages of the road to contemplation. It takes us from the domain of sounds to the affections of the mind, and then to a higher awareness which is simultaneously rational and supra-rational. Finally, we acquire a taste for the things of God, which amounts to being in communion with Him.

We will not fully explore the development of this theme, but once again, merely make a few reflections, this time on three aspects of Gregorian chant:

—The relationship between sensibility and intellect;

—The ethical dimension of music;

—The reciprocal relationship between man and God.

We feel confident that the notions explored previously concerning the liturgy and technique will aid us in our reflections.

The Relationship between Sensibility and Intellect

It is surely not heretical to say that union with God comes about through an act of charity—that is, through love, which presupposes an act of the intellect. But if we stop to consider this statement, a problem immediately arises concerning Gregorian chant, as well as every other kind of music; how, that is, can an art form, which makes such extensive use of our sensory perception, reach our intellect?

To begin with, it is inaccurate to say that art addresses only our senses, for it does not necessarily stop there. On the contrary, it should normally lead us beyond our senses.

Let us illustrate this point by tracing the work of a Gregorian composer. He chooses a text, usually from the Psalms, that lends itself to interpreting both an idea and a feeling or sentiment. These two aspects—thought and feeling—are inseparable. "Thought," said D. M. Sertillanges, "is always linked to sentiment."[1]

Because the word in a text resonates in the heart of the composer, he gives a form to his feeling, he marks his idea. He expresses in orderly fashion his understanding of the liturgical text. In this way the meaning of the text becomes richer and more intelligible.[2] To be sure, the chant adds nothing to the rational content of the message. But it puts it in a light that enhances intelligibility; it goes so far as to transcend the intellectual content of the message, thus bringing us into the realm of the inexpressible.[3]

After the composer has completed his task, the cantor and the listener, "sensitized" by the chant, are able to assimilate the message.

What has been said of the relationship between Gregorian chant and the liturgical text and of its technical characteristics suffices to show that the chant is better able than any other kind of music to serve as an intermediary between the senses and the intellect. As A. D. Sertillanges put it, "Its import is the most direct, because it is the closest to the idea."[4]

This brings up the value of Gregorian chant as a classic that transcends time. Its form, as a means of expression, is always contemporary; it expresses the noblest sentiments through its essential features. Because of this, it has an educational value which first touches our musical sense, and finally our entire being. As a corollary to these ideas, a Swiss musician once told us, "Gregorian chant is the model for every other form of music."

The Ethical Dimension of Music

At this point we could go on at length about the adage "art for art's sake," but suffice it to say that this cliché is radically anti-artistic. There are two kinds of music—one makes the listener the slave of what he or she hears, the other makes a person free. The first "casts a spell" over a man's sensual nature; the second is a work of the spirit. Recall for a moment the words of Gauguin: "Primitive art proceeds from the mind and makes use of nature . . . Nature debases the artist by letting itself be adored by him. . ."[5]

Gregorian chant does quite the opposite. Its prevailing mood has been described as a "calm state of excitement." Its pacifying and purifying character is a kind of moral preparation; its transparency wipes away the opaqueness of material things to open the way for spiritual values.[6] Pius XII, as well as other popes, has praised the holiness of Gregorian chant.[7] By holiness he meant the absence of foreign elements, and separation from the profane through consecration to God. True art reveals something of God's beauty, because man is created in the image and likeness of God. It opens the way into the realm of mystery, not only because it opens the soul to invisible and inexpressible mysteries, but because it renders these somehow tangible. Gregorian chant is a particularly effective instrument for touching the "ear of our heart."

One of the secrets of the effectiveness of the chant is that rather than striving to please the listener it speaks to him of God. People do not seek to find themselves in it, but to reach God. The musical art is eclipsed by the ultimate objective, which is union with God.

The Reciprocal Relationship between Man and God

After demonstrating that music separates us from both the world and our lower self, George Bàlan declared that music is not an end in itself, but opens us up to the mystical life. Thus it is supremely "Christ-like." For him this applied to "true music" as opposed to "anti-music," and above all to Gregorian chant.[8]

The word "Christ-like" invites the question whether Gregorian chant might not have a relationship with the Eternal Word, or, indeed, if it might not even possess an incarnational value of its own. We know, after all, of its intrinsic link with the Scriptures, and recognize that it speaks of God—or rather that God speaks of Himself to us—through the sung word. Bàlan thus verifies what A. D. Sertillanges expressed in a more general way. "What an honor," he said, "for this art to be so blended with the life of the soul in God, with the life of God in the soul."[9] Gregorian art appears to be more "mystical" than any other type of religious music.

Because it suggests and interprets divine realities, and because it inflames a disinterested love for these realities, the chant establishes a link between man and God. We could quote Saint Augustine, *"cantare amantis est,"* or "singing is a characteristic of the true lover," and then reverse it, *"amare cantoris est,"* or "loving is a characteristic of the singer." The place of love in Gregorian chant corresponds to the presence of the Holy Spirit in the soul. "If thou givest me peace, if thou givest me holy joy, then the soul of thy servant will be full of music," said Gerson, a sentiment taken up by St. Thomas à Kempis in his *Imitation of Christ.*[10]

The spiritual value of Gregorian chant is largely due to a religious experience undergone, successively, by the composer, the cantor, and the listener. In addition, Gregorian art, more than any other, reflects the good qualities of the artist—his artistic talent to be sure, but even more so his spiritual worth, his state of grace, his holiness. Gregorian chant has been compared to the art of making icons; there, the themes, prescribed to the slightest detail, allow the artist only to use his skill to express his soul, his inner life.

And so, in conclusion, let us return to the liturgical aspect of Gregorian chant and note how perfectly suited it is to the vertical part of the liturgy. Man serves as a mere instrument, but he is also a beneficiary. Like the liturgy itself, Gregorian chant is offered by Christ, the God-Man, unto the triune God, One and Three.

Conclusion

Many of these reflections, especially in the last part of this section, apply to any religious music worthy of the name. Even more broadly, many of the ideas that we have applied to Gregorian chant, though particularly apt to it, also serve for music in general. Our aim is not to reopen the old debate between Dom Gajard and Joseph Samson about the relative perfection, as sacred music, of Gregorian chant and polyphony.[11] Nor do we seek to contradict Rev. Father A. D. Sertillanges, O.P., who, with fine philosophical reasoning, concluded that the orchestra was best suited for religious music. We do not wish to dwell on comparisons. We simply want to understand why Gregorian chant deepens the spiritual life of so many people.

And what of the chant of the angels and the heavenly choruses mentioned at times in the lives of saints? Let us quote from the great English fourteenth-century mystic, Richard Rolle:

> It is not without reason that the lover of the Almighty is rapt to behold the highest things in the understanding and to sing hymns which give forth the most lovely sweetness of our Mediator, the songs of love that well up in the soul, ardently and unmistakably burned with the fire of love . . . Singing thus, he is led into every joy and he is altogether overcome and intoxicated with the force of the fervor which bursts forth and fills him with singular solace in this spiritual embrace and overwhelms him with intense ardor . . .
>
> The lover of the Godhead whose breast is wholly pierced with the love of the invisible beauty . . . shall receive within himself a sound sent from on high, his thoughts shall be turned to melody and his mind shall abide in marvelous music . . .
>
> . . . Rejoicing in Jesus I have taken flight from exterior to interior harmony . . . Hence the cry of my heart goes up, and my thought mingles as music amongst the songs of the heavenly citizens, seeking to reach up to the ears of the Most High.[12]

Gregorian chant can serve as an admirable prelude to these high mystical experiences.

Dare we go one step further? It is certain that one day you will come up against the disconcerting discovery that God is far above and beyond Gregorian chant. But, even then, you will have to admit that, second only to silence, Gregorian chant is a most excellent means for attaining God.

Endnotes

[1] Sertillanges, op. cit., p. 7.

[2] Cf. Hameline, op. cit., p. 34ff.

[3] Cf. Delalande, op. cit., p. 183. See also Charlier, op. cit., pp. 33 and 39.

[4] Sertillanges, op. cit., p. 21.

[5] Charles Morice, *Paul Gauguin*, Paris, 1920, quoted by Charlier, op. cit., p. 143.

[6] Cf. Sertillanges, Delalande.

[7] Pius XII, encyclicals, "Mediator Dei," November 20, 1947, and "Musicae sacrae disciplina," December 25, 1955.

[8] Bàlan, op. cit. pp. 317-318.

[9] Sertillanges, op. cit., p. 17.

[10] *The Imitation of Christ*, III, 50.

[11] Echoes of this can be found in J. Samson, "Music and Inner Life," Editions du Vieux Colombier, Paris, 1951, pp. 198-199.

[12] Richard Rolle, *The Fire of Divine Love*, translated by G. C. Heseltine, London, Burns Oates and Washbourne LTD, 1935.

6

Music and Spirituality

There is a profusion of books and articles bearing titles such as "Music and Spirituality." These writings vary in content, but most appear to have a common orientation. Although they differ with regard to the kinds of music they advocate, they generally concur in advocating high quality music. The differences increase when it comes to giving an exact definition of the word "spirituality." But they all wish to elevate the soul, and urge people to surpass even their highest capabilities.

This is a good place to quote Henri Davenson: "I plan to show that this music sows the seeds of Silence, serving as a technique of renunciation and inner purification. Consequently, for the sufficiently prepared soul, it becomes a means of asceticism, leading to contemplation."[1] The phenomenon of music can be analyzed at several levels. As a reality governed by the laws of acoustics, it falls into the domain of physics; as sound that affects our sense of hearing, it can be considered a physiological reaction.

Because music can affect our feelings or sentiments, it falls into the realm of psychology. And, beyond this, the mind, worked on by these feelings, forms value-judgments and ideas. In the end, the soul knows it has been enriched. All this is what we refer to when we talk about the spirituality of music, a spirituality that simultaneously involves feelings, value-judgments, and ideas.

The above describes music from the listener's viewpoint; he starts by perceiving the material aspect of the music, the sound, and then gradually becomes aware of its spiritual significance. Composers generally move in the reverse order; they begin with an emotional or idealistic inspiration which they proceed to express by creating musical forms. These forms act as links of communication and communion between minds. Hence we see that music is spiritual in its very essence.

Since these ideas are quite familiar, there is little need to dwell on them. We wanted only to recall them before presenting a few reflections on the spirituality of music and on all that the human soul puts into music.

We should, I believe, examine two matters: (1) music as a language of the spirit; and (2) the conditions required to make this language a reality.

Music, a Language of the Spirit

Every art has its own special language. Moreover, unlike mere technique, art is related to beauty. Technique, left to itself, aims only for utility, whereas art implies a love of beauty, the elevation of the soul, enchantment, rapture, and even a certain intimation of the divine.

Art is touched with the mark of freedom, a freedom that

does not exclude strict rules. It has a spontaneity entirely compatible with the disciplined labor of artistic creation. Its character is essentially gratuitous, even though it sometimes supports the artist. Artistic endeavors might be compared to the way a child plays, freely and spontaneously expressing himself through his game, and thus enriching his existence. But art, in addition, expresses an ideal, for the artist strives to fulfill his or her being by exteriorizing a dream conceived within the innermost self. What holds true for art in general applies in particular to music. Some would go even further and assert that music reflects an eternal model that is an echo of infinite Beauty.[2]

Hence it follows that music offers man a release from all things transitory—which does not entail an escape from reality. It is, rather, a means of purification. As listeners focus on the musical sounds that reach their ears, the never-ending flow of time takes on a significance for their inner lives. "The soul begins to feel luminous and transparent, with the awareness of being offered access to a new way of life . . . The soul thus grows truer to itself."[3]

Music is particularly apt for the role of purification since it expresses the inexpressible. To say that it supplements the spoken word, insufficient in itself, or that it is more subtle than words, would hardly suffice. For music adds nuances that words are simply incapable of expressing. It prompts us to enter a world which, in its own way, transcends the realm of concepts. As M. Zundel has written, it "uses and amplifies at will that living rhythm which, all alone, is able to restore to language the things that it lost in the process of conceptual abstraction: those concrete vibrations, those living and life-giving pulsations which normally go along with ideas."[4] .

Music draws us inward because it leads us, or perhaps we should say propels us, into a new world, the world of sound. Sound penetrates to the very center of our being, beyond the zone where feelings are formed, to the very seat of our knowledge and emotions.

Music has such infinite capacities for leading us towards spiritual realities, beyond any vision or precise feeling, that it has often been said that all true music is sacred. It makes us perceive, as it were, the infinite and eternal aspect of being. It puts us into communication with things divine. The Christian would say that it simultaneously *expresses* God and *leads us to* God. This indeed is the supreme requirement of all spirituality.

These reflections apply to music in general, or, if you prefer, "in the absolute." Now we must ask whether, on a concrete level, our conclusions hold true, or whether certain conditions have to be met before music can be an authentic language of the spirit.

Conditions for a Spiritual Language

Although music has a divine aspect, it also has an equally or even more important human dimension. The spiritual character of any piece will naturally be affected by the form chosen for it by the composer. The value of this form will depend, in turn, on the character of the artist, which necessarily infuses his created work. Its effectiveness will also vary according to the nature of the listener, who puts himself into the work he hears. We need, therefore, to consider first the musical form, and then the musician and the listener. But, since we are considering the spirituality of music, we will also reflect on God, Who is the ultimate objective.

Music

Musical forms are not all equally appropriate for conveying a spiritual message. Indeed, it is sometimes difficult to determine the exact point where mere noise ends and music begins. Noise itself can exert an influence over the soul. But can we really call that uplifting? In order for music to exist, the sounds must be organized in an orderly and harmonious manner.

Even among those sounds that can be called musical, several degrees and varieties exist. A military march will not affect the soul in the same way as a lullaby. "Light" music does not necessarily exclude art, and "great" music can sometimes be quite sensory.

But there is little point in attempting to classify musical forms according to their spiritual value. Such a classification would prove useless, since composers of differing temperaments tend to impart different characteristics to practically all the diverse forms. Nor would it get us very far to imagine, as a point of reference, a set of abstract principles defining a "universally valid classical art form" that was infallibly capable of reaching all hearts, and of carrying a universal, ever-relevant message. No single existing art form can pretend to have contributed to the spiritual growth of all people everywhere. Various types of music can claim to be spiritually uplifting, with certain capacities for universal appeal, but these qualities have never been monopolized by any one particular musical form.

A distinction needs to be made between types of music that can be referred to as spiritual, and others that might be called "sensual" or even "carnal." Music is said to be carnal when it awakens the purely animal instincts, inciting a prescribed set of physiological reactions, which in turn cause the individual or the group to behave in a pre-determined manner. Sensual music is superficial. It delights or "moves the listener," to quote Davenson, "more by the audible qualities of the sounds produced than by the essential spiritual significance that the overall composition takes on." As for spiritual music, it transcends the lower levels of being and deepens our spiritual self. And, in time, it tends to fade discreetly into the background, leaving the soul in "the heart of the most profound Silence."[5] Thus, music actually transcends itself.

The Musician and the Listener

Music involves a message. Its spiritual value, therefore, depends on the kind of message it carries, as well as on the qualities of both the artist who creates it and the listener who perceives it. Only someone with a penetrating soul can compose truly beautiful music—a perfect command of technique does not suffice. Therein lies the mystery of inspiration. "Talent" and "genius" indicate a person's capacity for sensing and expressing some profound idea in a powerful way.

Likewise, a soul must be penetrating to savor and comprehend music of high quality. We are given the music we deserve. We hear music and are enriched by it according to our receptive capacities. This in no way implies that music cannot educate or better people. On the contrary, it continually induces us to reach beyond our personal limits. But to do so, we must make a sincere effort to better ourselves. A person of good will can only grasp the spiritual message of music when he begins to deepen himself and to attain inner peace. Only in this way can he open himself up to the infinite, and rediscover the source from which all music flows.

And thus we see that music—at least a certain kind of music, the kind that can claim to be fundamentally spiritual—is never an end in itself. We can apply to it what someone wrote about Darius Milhaud: "Not a trace of narcissism, not an ounce of egocentrism."[6]

God

What ultimate goal are musicians striving to reach? Or, to broaden the question, what relationship is there between the musical and the mystical experience? According to the contemporary Rumanian philosopher George Bàlan, the musical and mystical domains are separate but intimately related; music acts as a preparation that leads to the very threshold of the mystical life.[7] Colling first insists upon the ways in which music and mysticism can be incompatible, but ends up seeing them as twin ways of approaching the infinite.[8] Davenson, drawing his inspiration from Saint Augustine, seems to adopt an even more positive and optimistic view: "Music amounts to something much more than a passing delight of the senses. It contains what might be referred to as the very root of eternal riches." Music does more than provide "a purely negative preparation for contemplation, a stripping of the soul of any encumbering obstacles. It actually leads us into Someone's Presence, it introduces us to One who knows us more intimately than we know ourselves. For some souls," Davenson concludes, "music is an inseparable part of the spiritual life."[9] Despite different shades of meaning, the outlook of these three authors converge on one and the same focal point—GOD.

Music uplifts the soul. If we respond with even the bare minimum of sensitivity and understanding, our hearts immediately gladden and open up, making us feel more authentically ourselves. At the same time we become aware that we are entering into another world. Our spirits, indeed our spiritual lives, are enriched.

For those of us who believe in God, this blossoming or enrichment of the heart encompasses communion with a personal, transcendent Being. Only then do we become fully aware of what the ultimate goal of music really is: a return to uncreated Beauty. This is something that others, nonbelievers, may perhaps only be able to sense in a vague, implicit manner.

If we are to delve beyond this point, we must refer to Christian theology. Christian doctrine is sometimes thought of as personal and subjective, enabling this or that musician to give expression to a particular type of spiritual message or form of sensitivity. But Christianity can also shed objective light on the very being of music. Christians hold that the world was created by the Blessed Trinity, and regenerated through the Incarnate Word, Jesus Christ, who offers an eternal song of praise to His Father. And the music of mankind has a mysterious but real share in this song. Not all are capable of grasping this reality, but we felt we should mention it here in concluding these "variations on the theme of music and spirituality."

Endnotes

[1] (See Bibliography): Davenson, op.cit., p.114.

[2] This is the particular point of view of Platonic philosophy, as seen by St. Augustine; cf. H. Davenson, op.cit., p. 17ff.

[3] J. Samson, "Music and Inner Life," Editions du Vieux Colombier, p. 151—cf. A. Colling, op.cit., p. 235.

[4] Maurice Zundel, op.cit., p. 359. The same idea was developed by Colling (op.cit., p. 116, quoting Bergson), etc.

[5] Davenson, op.cit., pp. 64 and 120.

[6] Paul Collaer, "Darius Milhaud. In celebration of his 80th Birthday" (*Orbis Musicae*, II, 1973-74, p. 8). Cf. Davenson, op.cit., p. 149. "It [music] must live in a soul who knows how to make good use of it, who instead of enjoying it as an illusory end in itself, makes use of it to draw closer to the only legitimate End, who is God."

[7] (See Bibliography): Bàlan, op. cit., pp. 314-315.

[8] (See Bibliography): Colling, op. cit., pp. 178-185.

[9] (See Bibliography): Davenson, op. cit., p. 79, pp. 130-137.

7

The Spirituality of the Liturgy

Of the various definitions of "the liturgy," two best suit our purpose here.

1. The liturgy is the public worship that the Church renders to God.

2. The liturgy is the praise that the Incarnate Word offers to His Father.

Both of these definitions are true, but neither of them is all-encompassing. Together, they intertwine and complement each other. A few theological explanations are perhaps in order.

God's perfect glory comes from Himself alone. It resides in the relationship that exists from all eternity among the three divine Persons of the Blessed Trinity, the unceasing exchange of mutual knowledge, love, and life among the Father, Son, and Holy Spirit. The created world, left to its own, could only offer God an extrinsic and imperfect kind of glory. It could do nothing more until the day when God, through the Incarnation, condescended to share in the condition of man whom He had created. This gave rise to a new form of glory which reached its consummation in Christ's sacrifice on the Cross and His Resurrection.

This same glory has since been perpetuated through the ministry of the Church, which was instituted by Christ for the purpose of extending the grace of his sacrifice to every place and age, in order to make it possible for all men to glorify God in a fitting manner.

The Incarnation of Christ, the Church, and the liturgy are all part of the same reality—hence the two definitions of the liturgy mentioned above. The first, which emphasizes public and official worship, implies a distinction between public and private prayer. Since the definition stresses the social aspect of the liturgy, it seems to minimize the equally indispensable aspect of individual and inner participation. But in reality, the true spirituality of the liturgy rests on the harmonious fusion of both these facets.

It is probably best not overly to press the distinction between public and private prayer. We need to remember that the Church exercises her public worship as the mystical body of Christ, and that when people take part in this social act, they are not inspired to do so primarily out of some vague "gregarious instinct," but as members of Christ, animated by the Holy Spirit. Each person retains his or her complete individual identity even in the midst of the largest liturgical assembly. The old saying about "worship being only as good as the worshipper" holds true, even in the midst of a crowd. Conversely, those engaged in a solitary form of life never cease to belong to an organized, structured community, the Church. Even a man like Charles de Foucauld,[1] when he went to live in his Sahara desert hermitage, continued to be a living and life-giving member of the Church.

The important thing is to understand correctly what is meant by the expression "liturgical spirituality," a term that can be used in two distinct but complementary ways. Its first meaning designates all the spiritual benefits that can be gleaned during the celebration of the liturgy through its various rites, its texts, its music, and more importantly through the "specific effect" it produces. This "effect" is the grace that God gives man through the sacraments. Sacramental grace enriches the soul in its very being and in its spiritual capacities. Theologians, in attempting to explain how this takes place, have said that God and the Church always offer grace in a complete and perfect way. But the reception of grace depends on the disposition of the person. This is important, because it explains why people benefit from the liturgy with varying intensity.

In its second meaning, the term "liturgical spirituality" depicts a Christian way of being, thinking, and acting as a result of participating in the liturgy. It describes how the liturgy can nourish our entire life, prolonging its effect far beyond the time spent in the actual worship service. This spirituality originates in the liturgy and flows from it. At the same time, it prepares and disposes the heart to participate more intensely in a future liturgy.

To sum up, "liturgical spirituality" can mean: (1) the actual celebration of the liturgy by Christ, and by all the faithful united to Christ as His members in the Mystical Body of the Church; (2) the way whereby the entire life of Christians is inspired, strengthened, and animated by the liturgy.

The first meaning concentrates on the social, cosmic, and eschatological dimensions of the liturgy, and on the central role of the mystical body of the faithful, united to Christ. The second stresses the good effected by the liturgy in the spiritual life of the individual person. Vatican II's "Constitution on the Sacred Liturgy," which describes the liturgy as the "summit and source [*culmen et fons*] of the Church's life" (no.10), links these two meanings. It emphasizes the first, the collective aspect, and shows how the second, the individual dimension, flows from it. The document deserves lengthy quotation:

> The liturgy is rightly considered to be the exercise of Jesus Christ's priestly office . . . in which the fullness of public worship is accomplished by the Mystical Body of Jesus Christ, that is, by the Head and His members.
>
> From this it follows that every liturgical celebration, because it is an action of Christ the priest and His Body which is the Church, is a sacred action surpassing all others; no other action of the Church can either claim to have, or actually achieve, so advanced a degree of efficacy.
>
> In the earthly liturgy we participate in a foretaste of that heavenly liturgy which is celebrated in the holy city of Jerusalem toward which we journey as pilgrims, where Christ is sitting at the right hand of God, a minister of the holy sanctuary and the true tabernacle; (Rev 21:2; Col 3:1; Heb 8:2); with the entire army of heavenly hosts, we sing to the Lord a hymn of glory; venerating the memory of the saints, we hope for some part and fellowship with them; we eagerly await the Savior, Our Lord Jesus Christ, until He, our life, shall appear and we too will appear with Him in glory.
>
> The sacred liturgy does not absorb the entire activity of the Church. . . . (The preliminary work of preaching

the Gospel message and instructing the faithful is also essential).

. . . Nevertheless, the liturgy is the summit toward which the activity of the Church is directed; at the same time it is the source from which all her power flows. For the aim and object of apostolic works is that all who are made sons of God by faith and baptism should come together to praise God in the midst of His Church, to take part in the sacrifice, and to eat the Lord's supper.

The liturgy in its turn moves the faithful, filled with the paschal sacraments, to be "one in holiness"; it prays that "they may hold fast in their lives to what they have grasped by their faith"; the renewal in the Eucharist of the covenant between the Lord and man draws the faithful into the compelling love of Christ, and sets them on fire. From the liturgy, therefore, and especially from the Eucharist, as from a font, grace is poured forth upon us; and the sanctification of men in Christ and the glorification of God, to which all other activities of the Church are directed as toward their goal, is achieved in the most efficacious way possible.

But in order that the liturgy may be able to produce its full effects, it is necessary that the faithful come to it with the correct spiritual dispositions, that their minds should be attuned to their voices, and that they should cooperate with divine grace lest they receive it in vain.[2]

Thus, having learned of the relationship between liturgy as a social act of the Church, and the ways in which it affects the spiritual life of each Christian, we come to the following conclusion:

1. The liturgy nourishes and deepens the spiritual life

of the Church as a whole, and of each individual member. Participation in the external rites and in the song of the liturgy is not meant to be an end in itself, to be achieved at all costs, but rather to bring the faithful to communion with the great invisible realities of Christianity, or to give an authentic expression to that communion. In the domain of sacred music, Gregorian chant is best adapted to this ultimate goal.

2. The more authentic the spiritual life of each member, the more perfect the liturgy. For "the rites and forms that the Church employs in her liturgy would have no value if they were not the expression of an inner and spiritual worship."[3] To repeat a familiar adage which sums up a thought often expressed by St. Augustine through his commentaries on the Psalms: *"Laus cantandi est ipse cantator"* ("The chant's worth is measured by the worth of the singer." Or, better still: "The singer himself (ipse cantator) is the praise of the One whom the song is meant to celebrate (laus cantandi").[4]

This brings us to the contemplative dimension of the liturgy. Dom Guéranger, renowned for his insistence on the primordial place of the liturgy in Christian spirituality, put it plainly: "Liturgy," he would say, "*is* contemplation." One of Dom Guéranger's greatest disciples, Madame Cécile Bruyère, first abbess of Solesmes's monastery of Benedictine nuns, developed this theme by describing the interaction between the celebration of the Divine Office and contemplative prayer: "By a double current, which consists in praying mentally the better to celebrate the Divine Office, and in seeking in the Divine Office food for mental prayer, the soul gently, quietly, and almost without effort arrives at true contemplation."[5] Madame Bruyère tended to identify